Woodworking

Essentials

Beginner's Guide to the Basics and the Right Tools and Techniques for Woodworking Projects

By Charlie Mandler

© **Copyright 2020 - All rights reserved.**

The content contained within this book may not be reproduced, duplicated or transmitted without direct written permission from the author or the publisher.

Under no circumstances will any blame or legal responsibility be held against the publisher or author for any damages, reparation, or monetary loss due to the information contained within this book. Either directly or indirectly.

Legal Notice:

This book is copyright protected. This book is only for personal use. You cannot amend, distribute, sell, use, quote or paraphrase any part, or the content within this book, without the consent of the author or publisher.

Disclaimer Notice:

Please note the information contained within this document is for educational and entertainment purposes only. All effort has been executed to present accurate, up to date and reliable, complete information. No warranties of any kind are declared or implied. Readers acknowledge that the author is not engaging in the rendering of legal, financial, medical or professional advice. The content within this book has been derived from various sources. Please consult a licensed professional before attempting any techniques outlined in this book.

By reading this document, the reader agrees that under no

circumstances is the author responsible for any losses, direct or indirect, which are incurred as a result of the use of information contained within this document, including, but not limited to, —errors, omissions, or inaccuracies.

Contents

INTRODUCTION 1

Chapter 1: Your Space 5

Chapter 2: Starting Toolbox 8

Chapter 3: Looking After Your Woodworking Tools 20

Chapter 4: Woodworking Glossary 24

Chapter 5: Choosing Your Wood 33

Chapter 6: Shop Safety 42

Chapter 7: Typical Mistakes 47

Chapter 8: Joints 50

    Butt Joints 50

    Dowel Joints 51

    Dovetail Joints 53

    Slotted Tenon Joints 56

Chapter 9: Starting With Your Journey 58

    Storage Chest 59

    A Workbench 63

Chapter 10: What if Something Goes Wrong 69

CONCLUSION 72

Thank you for buying this book and I hope that you will find it useful. If you will want to share your thoughts on this book, you can do so by leaving a review on the Amazon page, it helps me out a lot.

INTRODUCTION

So you wish to learn woodworking? Woodworking could be an enjoyable and pleasing pastime, however, it can additionally be rather discouraging. In a world filled with mass-produced, inadequately crafted furniture pieces, it could be a thrill to produce a piece made with your own two hands.

Take a couple of pieces of wood, some tools, and your creativity, and you can make gorgeous furniture pieces. The possibilities of woodworking are limitless. Even the most unskilled individual can learn woodworking and turn out beautiful pieces that can end up being treasures.

Woodworking as a pastime is growing in appeal-- specifically amongst the female population. A growing number of ladies are taking a brand-new interest in jigsaws and power drills as they turn out accessories and furnishings for their houses.

The term "woodworking" actually describes the procedure of building, making, or carving something utilizing wood. Sort of apparent, isn't it? However, there are all kinds of pieces that could be made using wood-- not simply furnishings! You can make toys, toy boxes, or carved figurines. It can genuinely end up being an art form.

So where and how does a hopeful woodworker start? Lots of people benefit considerably from taking a class at the local college or community center. Others choose to read a book or publication. Still, others choose to leap right in. There's no one appropriate way to begin. It depends upon just how much experience you have with utilizing the tools necessary for woodworking.

Woodworking is not as challenging as it might appear. It is not required to spend a fortune on tools and materials. Lots of tasks could be performed with a minimum financial investment and your creativity!

Woodworking is a substantial pastime, with a variety of active participants. Each person brings their own set of abilities and interests that frequently make particular methods more relevant in their situation. As long as the methods are safe, and produce the wanted outcomes, they are right for them.

This book is about introducing you to fundamental woodworking terms, beginning with an equipped shop, carving out your work area, and introducing you to some fundamental woodworking jobs. We are going to focus primarily in here on building furniture pieces. When you master this, you can get more thorough with carving as you discover how to utilize your tools better.

This is not a thorough, conclusive guide, however, it is a great way to get going with crafting your own projects and discovering the complete satisfaction of making your own furnishings, toys, and a lot more!

I have actually featured a part about shop safety, and some simple projects to get you started!

So let's begin with this guide to woodworking!

Chapter 1: Your Space

The first thing you want to think about is where you'll be crafting your projects. Many people take up woodworking in their garage or basement. This is good; simply bear in mind that you'll require some area to store components and the finished item. You'll desire an area that is simple to move around in which you can remain organized.

If you're utilizing power tools, you'll require quickly accessible power outlets. Keep in mind that power tools could be rather loud, so take into account the convenience of your family and your next-door neighbors.

You'll require a workbench which does not always need to be intricate. It's an area for you to work on and keep your plans out in the open.

You can purchase commercially made workbenches at most house supply shops. When picking a workbench, try to find one with a wood top, or another smooth, non-marking top, so that the surface does not scuff the wood you utilize for your projects. Storage below the bench is nice if your budget plan enables a model with integrated drawers and cabinets.

Select a workbench that fits conveniently in your store area, which matches the kinds of projects you believe you'll be working on. A little workbench is going to do for crafting toys, however, you'll require a bigger area if you're making armoires.

However, you're starting with woodworking as a pastime. Why not make your own workbench? This is going to provide you with important experience and is going to turn into one of the most helpful items in your store! I have included an easy workbench plan in this book. Attempt diving right in and kick off your workshop with a piece you made yourself!

It's a great idea to have a bin where you can position operating handbooks from your tools. By doing this, you will not lose them, and they'll be quickly accessible.

I additionally suggest an excellent tool kit to keep your tools and a box like a tackle box to keep nails and screws in.

Just like the majority of any projects, the better arranged you are, the more effective you'll be. You'll additionally conserve yourself a great deal of tension by having the ability to find what you require quickly.

Some individuals like to have a pegboard over their workbench to hang their tools on. This is an excellent idea, just as having a bulletin board system so you can hang the plans for your existing project.

Lastly, you'll require excellent lighting. You can get store lights cheaply at discount stores like Wal-Mart or Home Depot.

Now that you have a place to work, what do you require to start? The apparent answer would be wood, which we'll discuss a little later. What's the 2nd apparent answer? Tools!

Chapter 2: Starting Toolbox

If you intend to make woodworking into a pastime for a very long time, you're much better off purchasing great tools rather than the more affordable ones. They'll hold up much better and last longer.

As far as hand tools are concerned, you'll be fine purchasing used older ones as long as they remain in good condition. The quality of older tools has a tendency to be much better and they're made to last.

You can construct quality projects with just hand tools, however, power tools make the job a lot simpler. Be particularly leery of purchasing used or marked down power tools. Ensure they are safe and work successfully.

You do not need to rush out and purchase everything at one time. This is a pastime that can make you cash, which could be utilized to purchase tools. It might even develop into a livelihood if you do a good enough job!

When you get the word out to family and friends that you are diving into woodworking, a great deal of them might have excess tools lying around that you can utilize. Reward any generosity with a lovely piece once you start!

The following are the standard tools you'll require.

Claw hammers are the most typical kinds of hammers utilized for woodworking and basic repairs around the house. They are offered with various kinds of handles, wood, steel with rubber or plastic grips, and fiberglass composition. The style of hammer you choose ought to be an individual choice, hold the hammer in your hand as if to strike a nail, it ought to feel well balanced, the grip ought to be comfortable. There are various weights. 16 ounces is an excellent general-purpose option, while for heavier things, 20 ounces is more appropriate. Tinier weights are appropriate for tacks and light work or kids.

Screwdrivers are required for nearly every woodworking project. Make certain you have numerous sizes of both Phillips head and flat head screwdrivers. I'm particularly keen on my cordless, electric screwdriver that includes various size bits for all kinds of projects. In this manner, I have one tool with the flexibility of ten of them!

Wood chisels vary in size from 1/4" to 2" wide in 1/8" graduations. They are available with wood or plastic handles. Utilize a chisel about one half the width of the cut to be made. Thin cuts could be made by pressing by hand; much heavier cuts are made by tapping on the end with a wood mallet. You'll desire a number of various sizes of chisels-- no requirement to purchase all sizes when you're simply beginning!

Levels are available in numerous shapes and sizes, the most typical being 24" long. They could be made from wood, aluminum or plastic. Some have actually fixed vials. Others are adjustable. All levels have several vials for vertical and horizontal usage. Some have 45-degree vials. Inside the vial is a fluid with an air bubble. When the bubble is focused between the two indicator lines, the surface is level.

You'll require a level to guarantee that your project ends up straight. You do not wish to develop a bookshelf just to see it noted at a 45-degree angle!

Framing Squares are essential in woodworking. With this tool, it is possible to design and determine almost everything in the construction of a home from the basement stairs up to the attic rafters. It might additionally be described as a steel square or a carpenter's square. The most typical size has a 24" blade and a 16" tongue. Nevertheless, there are tinier sizes available, yet like some more affordable variations of the bigger style, they do not have the framing tables stamped on them.

Try Square - These squares have a steel tongue fixed into a wood handle, they vary in size from 3" to 12", some have inch scales on them, and others are blank. They are really helpful for furnishings and cabinet making as they are little enough to suit confined areas.

Triangles - These are available in numerous sizes and shapes in different products. The double 45 ° and a 30 °- 60 ° are the two shapes utilized most in laying out patterns.

A measuring tape can be found in a variety of widths and lengths. I would not advise anything less than 3/4" wide for a tape over 6 feet long as they can not be extended out and stay rigid. For little projects in the shop, 1/2" wide ones are adequate. Some have actually highlighted signs at each foot; others have them at 16-inch periods, which is handier in construction for stud layout, whereas the foot indications are better in the shop. Special tapes are available for lefties in addition to ones with digital read-outs. The hook on the end is to be loose so that it offers precise measurement, whether it is hooked over the edge or butted up to an edge. Examine if the hook has actually been bent if measurements are not precise.

Nail and Screws-- you can purchase these as required for numerous projects, however, you ought to still keep on hand numerous sizes of nails and screws.

Sandpaper-- You'll utilize a great deal of sandpaper in completing your projects. Have different grades offered for the various projects you'll be finishing. Fine grit paper is utilized for the majority of wood projects. Medium is usually utilized for the initial sanding of softwoods and shaping. Coarse grit ought to be utilized for paint removal, rough sanding, and shaping.

Various Saws-- A fret saw utilizes extremely narrow blades so that elaborate designs could be cut. The blade could be turned a complete 360 ° for tight corners. Inside cuts are started by drilling a little hole to make it possible for the blade to go through it. Then the blade is placed into the saw frame. Deepthroated saws, called scroll saws, with frames having 18" clearance are readily available. Handsaws are offered in numerous sizes and setups; an excellent general purpose saw is 26" long and has 8 teeth per inch. Crosscut saws (to cut across the grain) have teeth with a negative rake; ripping saws (to cut in the direction of the grain) have a zero rake.

Hand Plane - There are various styles of hand planes, and some are made from steel, while others are made from wood. Many are made to smooth the surface area. There are some with blades created to cut profiles; however, with the arrival of the router, these are less typical. Squaring up board edges and tidying up rough boards is simple to do with a hand plane. While you just require a standard smoothing plane to take on most projects, don't buy the least expensive hand plane you discover. Search for a brand name or at least good quality metal to make sure the plane is going to last a very long time.

Clamps - Any project that is glued needs clamping to make sure that the parts are bonded securely in precisely the appropriate position. You can never ever have excessive clamps. It is an excellent idea to get any that are available for a great fee, particularly at swap meets and yard sale, no matter what style they are.

You'll utilize clamps to glue boards side to side and to hold projects together as joints dry. Purchasing pipe clamps that vary from 18 inches to 8 feet wide ought to guarantee you have the appropriate clamp for the majority of projects. Include a couple of hand clamps and little C-clamps for tinier jobs, too. If you intend to deal with oak a lot, think about purchasing pipe clamps with zinc-coated pipelines to stop staining of the wood.

Vises-- A vise holds wood pieces steady on the workbench as you form them with other tools. A mid-size vise, with a 7- to 9-inch opening, suffices for a novice. Try to find a vise with wood jaws or inserts, or utilize smooth scrap wood to maintain the vise from denting your projects.

Rasps - Rough metal rasps are utilized to file board edges and get rid of smidgens of wood. Two rasps, one fine and one coarse, ought to be all you require

Electric Drill and Drill Bits - Electric drills are, without a doubt, the very first power tool acquired. They have many usages besides drilling holes. There are attachments to turn them into paint mixers, sanders, screwdrivers, saws, mills, lathes, and the list goes on.

There are corded and cordless drills, and each one has its time and place. I would advise beginning with a 3/8" capability, variable speed, reversible corded drill. It is not going to be as useful as cordless, however, you are going to get great performance for a low price.

Select a slower speed model, (max. 1200 rpm), they appear to have more torque for drilling bigger holes yet still drill tidy tinier holes. A lot of drills are now double insulated, which is a security aspect. If it has a three-prong plug, utilize a three-prong extension cable.

Electric Circular Saw-- These could be extremely useful when cutting your wood pieces. No requirement to spend a lot on this, nevertheless. Locate one that's simple for you to utilize and dependable.

Jig Saw-- While not entirely needed, a great jigsaw can assist make your woodworking tasks simpler. They can add some appealing details to a piece and make cutting wood simpler too.

Router - Routers have actually turned into one of the most used tools in a workshop, potentially a lot more popular than a table saw. A fully equipped store is going to have both a plunge base and a fixed base router; it is now possible to get a mixed package where one device has both bases.

There are several bit profiles available. Most likely, a straight bit and a round-over bit are the very first ones you are going to require, however, this depends upon the kind of projects you are going to be doing. It is a lot easier to deal with tinier pieces if the router is installed on a table. Typically, better outcomes are accomplished by taking a number of passes making shallow cuts, instead of one pass if a great deal of material needs to be removed.

Glue-- You'll desire to have some strong carpenter's wood glue on hand to guarantee your piece's stability.

Carpenter's Pencil - Rectangular-shaped pencil, about 1/4" X 1/2", with a 1/16" X 3/16" lead.

Keep safety glasses at hand, even if you aren't utilizing power tools in your woodshop. When utilizing a hammer or moving boards, things or wood shavings can fly up rapidly, putting you at risk of injury.

A standard first aid kit ought to additionally be readily available for store accidents, though you can considerably decrease your threat of woodshop accidents by constantly utilizing your hand tools as they are meant. Utilizing the appropriate tool for the task conserves wear and tear on the tools and on you.

Lastly, keep a wet/dry store vacuum close by so that you can rapidly tidy up wood shavings and dust. Keeping dust and wood particles to a minimum is going to lower the danger of woodshop fires and assist you to breathe easier, too.

I'll presume you have a standard understanding of using a hammer and screwdriver. If you are going to be utilizing power tools, simply count on the guide that is going to come with it if you purchase it brand-new. If you don't purchase it brand-new, get the assistance of a member of the family or buddy to show you. A last-ditch resort is to check out the Web or get a book from your public library. Utilizing tools isn't brain surgery. They're quite simple to figure out if you put in the time. Simply keep in mind to be cautious and practice safe usage.

What do you have to learn about utilizing mechanical tools? Continue reading!

Chapter 3: Looking After Your Woodworking Tools

A couple of things are more interesting than getting a brand-new power tool! After conserving the cash, doing the research study, and all the relative shopping, getting the package and calling it your own feels great.

Devices: they are going to cut, they are going to drill, and they are going to flatten or slice nearly anything. However, you need to look after them. Read and comprehend the owner's handbook, then keep it for later reference. When a device is established, it still has to be inspected regularly for positioning, for bolts requiring tightening, lubrication, and cleaning.

Learn to 'tune' each device within its tolerances: band saw wheels have to run in the identical plane, a drill press has to raise and lower vertically square to its table, and a table saw blade needs to be ninety degrees square to its tabletop, with the front and back of the blade running parallel to its miter slots.

Books are an excellent source of information of this kind.

Before you pack a motor with heavy use, enable it to develop to full force so it can do its task effectively. New devices, specifically, require to be enabled to run a number of minutes before heavy usage the first time, to enable the brushes in the motor to 'seat.' Learn the noise of the motor on each device, and take notice of how it sounds under a load of operation. If something's incorrect, you'll frequently have the ability to hear or feel it from the device before things go wrong.

Do not attempt to work any device too quickly. If a procedure takes too much force, something is most likely wrong, like hardened wood or not ample chip clearance for a blade, or misalignment of vital parts. If you feel the work is overtaxing the device, discover another way to do it, or divide the task into tinier steps.

Know beforehand where your 'panic button' is. Practice holding the workpiece clear of the blade, then turn the device on and off. Before you start, understand where that off-switch is, and understand how you are going to get to it. There are after-market aids to make off-buttons accessible by your knee instead of fumbling for it by hand.

Constantly unplug a device when dealing with or changing blades. Not just can bumping a switch offer you a nasty surprise, however, defective switches (even the 'safer' magnetic switches) have actually been known to link and come on with an abrupt blow to a tabletop, like a dropped tool or piece of wood. If there is a power blackout, disconnect each device separately and leave the lights on to inform you when the power has actually been brought back.

Keep your devices tidy. Vacuum the dust out of motor vents, off belts, switches, pulleys and inside router collets. Keep band saw tires tidy with a toothbrush and isopropyl alcohol, turning the wheels by hand. If you have a rack and pinion height modification, make sure its teeth and gears are kept devoid of sawdust accumulation.

As a rule, see that your workpiece is firmly clamped in place or directed as it passes a blade. Never ever cut freehand on a table saw; support the workpiece versus a fence or miter gauge, however, do not utilize the two together since that might bind the workpiece versus the blade and trigger a nasty kickback or jamming of the blade. A panel-cutting sled riding in the miter slot is the best method to do cross-cuts. With portable power tools, before you start, plan how the electrical cable is going to pass easily as you finish the operation, and if your cable is of sufficient length (this is one terrific benefit of battery-operated tools.) Be sure a cable isn't going to snag on something needlessly or coil around your feet. The very best guidance on brand-new machinery is to inform yourself and practice before you start the work. Woodworking is a fantastic pastime, however, you are accountable for your own wellbeing.

So now you're equipped and have guidance on your tools. Let's take a look at some woodworking terms you may not recognize yet.

Chapter 4: Woodworking Glossary

- Adhesive - A compound that can bond the material together by surface area accessory.

- Air Dried - Lumber stacked and saved so that it is dried naturally by the direct exposure to air.

- Allen Head - A screw head with a recess needing a hexagon-shaped secret, utilized primarily on equipment. These might remain in metric or SAE sizes.

- Apron - This is a frame around the base of a table to which the top and legs are attached.

- Bench Dogs - Pegs that enter into holes in the top of a workbench that deal with a vise to hold broad material.

- Biscuit Joint - An oval-shaped disk that when placed in a slot with glue swells to form a tight bond. A special tool is needed to cut the slot.

- Block Airplane - A little plane developed for cutting across the end grain.

- Board Foot - Measurement of lumber equal to one square foot, which is an inch thick or 144 cubic inches. Multiply width in inches X length in inches X density in inches, and divide by 144 for overall board feet.

- Box Joint - Square-shaped finger joints utilized to join pieces at correct angles.

- Butt Joint - A joint where the edges of 2 boards are against one another.

- Caliper - An instrument with 2 legs, with one of them moving, utilized to determine the density of items.

- Chuck - An accessory to hold work or a tool in a device. Lathe chucks and drill chucks are instances of this.

- Compound Miter - An angled cut to both the edge and face of a board. The most typical usage is with crown molding.

- CrossCut - A cut that runs across the board perpendicular to the grain.

- Dado - A groove in the face of a board, generally to accept another board at 90 degrees as in shelf uprights.

- Dovetail Joint - A joint where the fingers are formed like a doves tail, utilized to join pieces at 90 degrees.

- Dowel - A wood pin utilized to line up and hold 2 adjacent pieces.

- Dowel Center - Metal buttons that enter into a predrilled dowel hole to mark the position for drilling the second piece.

- Epoxy Glue - A two-part glue that virtually glues anything to anything.

- European Hinge - A concealed style hinge attached to the door with a cup hole.

- Filler - A compound that is utilized the fill pores and abnormalities on the surface of the component to reduce the porosity prior to using a finishing coat.

- Finger Joint - Long tapered fingers utilized to join material lengthwise, typically utilized in making molding to join brief lengths.

- Grain - The look, size, and direction of the positioning of the fibers of the wood.

- Hand Plane - A tool to smooth and real wood surfaces, including a blade attached in the frame at an angle with hand grips to move it along the board.

- Jig - A tool utilized to hold work or serve as a guide in production or assembly.

- Joiner - A device utilized to true the edges of boards, typically to prepare for gluing.

- Kerf - The width of a saw cut determined by the density and set of the blade.

- Kick Back - This is when a workpiece is thrown back by a cutter, prevented by utilizing anti-kickback tools on power tools like table saws.

- MDF - Medium-Density Fiberboard, extremely steady underlay for countertops to be covered with laminate

- Miter Box - A device to assist a saw in making miter joints.

- Miter Gauge - A guide with an adjustable head that suits a slot and slides across a power tool table to cut component at an angle.

- Miter Joint - Pieces are cut at an angle to create a joint.

- Molding (Moulding) - A strip of the component with a profile cut on the facing edges, utilized for trimming.

- Ogee - An S shape that is created by creating one cut to generate 2 similar pieces.

- Particle Board - A generic term for component made from wood particles and bound together with glue

- Plumb - A term utilized to illustrate something that is completely perpendicular to the earth relative to gravity. A plumb bob on the end of a string is going to provide you with a line that is plumb or directly up and down.

- Plywood - A glued wood panel generally 4' X 8' comprised of thin layers of wood, laid at appropriate angles to one another.

- Rip Cut - A cut that goes through the length of a board alongside the grain.

- Sawhorse - A trestle typically utilized in sets to hold wood for cutting.

- Spline - A thin strip of wood fitted between 2 grooves to create a joint.

- T - slot - A slot grated in the shape of an upside-down T to hold special bolts for clamps or jigs.

- Table Saw - A circular saw installed under a table with height and angle changes for the blade.

- Taper Cut - A cut where the width goes down from one end to the other. These are generally done on a table saw with a jig.

- Tear out - The propensity to splinter the tracking edge of the component when cutting across the grain.

- Template - A pattern to direct the marking or cutting of shape, typically a router is utilized with a piloted bit.

- Tenon - A projection created by removing the wood around it to place it into a mortise to make a joint.

- Tongue and Groove - A joinery approach where a board has an extending tongue on one edge, and a groove on the other. The tongue of one board fits into the groove of the next.

- Witness Marks - These are marks placed on boards or pieces to keep them in order throughout gluing, joining, and assembly.

- X-Acto Knife - This is a razor-like blade in a handle; the blades are available in numerous shapes, really useful for great work.

There are a lot of various terms utilized in woodworking. The above is definitely just a partial list. You are going to find yourself discovering the terms as you end up being increasingly more acquainted with the world of woodworking and carpentry.

When you take part in the world of woodworking, there's something you merely can not do without-- wood!

Chapter 5: Choosing Your Wood

The two standard categories of wood are wood and softwood. There is also created wood like plywood.

What you utilize for any given job depends upon numerous elements: strength, solidity, grain qualities, expense, stability, weight, color, sturdiness, and availability. Normally, starting woodworkers begin with softwood like pine. It's soft and simple to work with, and you do not require costly tools to get excellent outcomes. It is offered at local lumberyards and house centers. It has its restrictions when it comes to creating furniture. It is a softwood and is going to get damaged quickly.

Softwood is from an evergreen or coniferous (cone-bearing) tree. Typical ranges are pine, fir, spruce, hemlock, cedar and redwood. These woods are primarily utilized in the house construction market. Cedar and redwood are exceptional options for outside projects, while pine is frequently utilized for "Early American Country Design" furnishings.

Pine and most other softwoods are going to soak up and lose moisture more than hardwoods, so they are not as steady. Buy the lumber at least 2 weeks prior to beginning your project and keep it inside.

You are going to discover that softwoods are offered in basic density and widths. For instance, a 1 X 4 is going to be 3/4" thick and 3 1/2" wide comparable to construction components. The product is going to typically be priced per lineal foot, and the price is going to increase appropriately for the wider boards.

Hardwood lumber originates from deciduous trees, the ones that shed their leaves each year. Popular domestic types are oak, maple, cherry, birch, walnut, ash, and poplar. Of these typical native hardwoods, just red oak and poplar are normally stocked in house centers and lumberyards. The others need to be acquired from specialized shops. The product stocked at home centers and lumberyards are normally offered in comparable dimensions to softwood and by the lineal foot also.

At specialty shops, the density of hardwood lumber is specified in quarters of an inch, measured when the wood remains in a rough state. The thinnest stock is 4/4, and the thickest normally offered is 16/4. Instead of being grated to defined measurements, like pine, hardwoods are offered in random widths and lengths.

Dealing with hardwoods is rather different from dealing with pine; you can not drive a screw through hardwood lumber without first tiring a pilot hole. Cutting and planing hardwoods need incredibly sharp tools.

Hardwoods are excellent to utilize when developing furnishings. Oak and ash are referred to as open-grain woods. These species have changing parts of reasonably permeable and thick wood. When stained, the open-grain parts soak up the color easily while the more difficult parts are more resistant. This highlights the grain patterns, producing a remarkable result.

Cherry, maple and birch are closed-grain woods, showing a more consistent texture throughout a board. Poplar is additionally a closed-grain wood, however, its color varies from a beige to olive green, and typically has actually purple highlights tossed into the mix. Due to this uncommon coloration, it is seldom utilized if a furnishings piece is going to have a clear finish. This wood is best when stained or painted. Poplar, being less costly, is additionally a great option for framing hardwood tasks.

Hardwood is more long-lasting and less susceptible to dents and scratches. It is additionally more costly, however, it is going to finish to a much better degree. Softwoods, like pine, are more susceptible to dents and scratches and do not have the toughness of hardwood. Softwoods are much less costly and simpler to discover. Ask your lumber provider to show you "Class 1" or "Select Grade" lumber. Ensure it is effectively dried, and without knots and problems. (It might be unlikely to be entirely devoid of flaws, however, make sure you comprehend how to cut around these).

The two most typically made sheets products utilized in furnishings making are MDF (Medium Density Fiberboard) and Particle Board. Both are made from wood particles, combined with glue and bonded under pressure. MDF has finer particles than Particle Board, so it produces a smoother and more powerful item.

MDF works effectively and is frequently utilized for molded elements on painted furnishings. Its primary downside is that it is really heavy compared to actual wood.

Due to their laminated building, they are very steady in all measurements. Given that the veneers on any provided panel are generally cut sequentially from the identical log, the panel ought to show a uniform color and grain. Matching the grain pattern of strong wood to the typically uniform grain pattern on the panels could be tough. However, patient preparation can yield excellent matches in the most noticeable parts of your task.

Manufactured sheets do have restrictions. Whenever they are utilized, no matter the core, the edge needs to be concealed, and the veneers on the surface are very thin, frequently less than 1/32 in. Due to this, the surface area is vulnerable and tends to divide out, specifically on the rear of a saw cut. Additionally, given that the veneer is so thin, aggressive sanding can rapidly work through the veneer and expose the unsightly core beneath.

As we stated, what wood you utilize depends upon what type of project you are carrying out. For projects that are going to be painted, you can utilize merely MVF. For furnishings, it's frequently an excellent idea to pick something that is going to finish well, like cedar or oak.

You'll more than likely be getting your wood from a lumber supply shop or a home enhancement shop like Home Depot or Lowe's. There are a couple of things you want to bear in mind when choosing your lumber.

At the lumber yard or shop, you'll discover wood boards stacked up in high stacks according to length, quality grade, density, wood type and numerous other classifications. Even in stacks of boards that are organized as being the same, there are distinctions in quality, so follow these easy ideas for selecting boards that are going to work for your woodworking projects.

Do not take boards you do not desire! Lumberyard beginners might feel like they need to take the boards that are first provided to them. Do not hesitate to take a look at each board carefully and send boards back if they do not satisfy your requirements. Why pay for a deformed board that will not work in your project? Turning down boards is not an insult, it is a way to pay for wood you can utilize, so get in the habit early.

Look for straightness. Hold the board at eye level on one end, with the other end on the ground. Look down the board to see if it has apparent curves or twists. Some projects can manage a curved board; however, for novices, dealing with curved boards might be too convoluted.

Look for splits and warping. Examine both sides of the board to see if there are any long splits or deformed edges. Splits and warps lower the quantity of wood you can utilize for your project, so pass on boards that would lead to a great deal of waste.

Knotholes could be considered appealing in some types of woodworking projects, so if you're trying to find a truly knotty piece of wood, that's fine. Otherwise, inspect your boards for big knotholes that would end up being waste wood or loose knot pieces that might fall out, triggering gaps or weak parts in your cut pieces. For great woodworking projects or projects that require a straight, even grain, quarter sawn lumber provides even wood graining, however, it is more pricey than routine plain-sawn lumber. Choose whether you want to pay for the straight grain prior to selecting boards.

Look carefully at each board to see if the color is even enough for your project and that there are not a great deal of wormholes or other marred parts. Additionally, look for lumberyard chalk or pen markings or dents that might not come off quickly.

Used boards collected from old barns or other projects could be fascinating and enjoyable to deal with. Nevertheless, when purchasing or picking recovered lumber, look for indications of decay. If the board is spongy or soft or has indications of fungi on it, it might not hold up well as project wood.

Pressure-treated lumber and chemically-treated lumber are for usage in outside projects and are much better able to endure temperature level and wetness alterations. If you're developing a deck or outside project, request treated lumber. Otherwise, untreated boards are a much better option.

The starting woodworker ought to most likely begin utilizing softer woods like pine or spruce. They are simpler to work with, and you can ultimately move up to more difficult woods like oak and cedar. You're nearly prepared to start, however initially, let's evaluate some security procedures all excellent woodworkers comply with.

Chapter 6: Shop Safety

When you are working around sharp saws, machinery that can sever a limb, and heavy boards, it is necessary to be safe and prevent any oversights that might threaten your health and even your life!

Safety glasses or goggles ought to be used whenever power tools remain in usage and when sculpting, sanding, scraping or hammering overhead. This is really crucial for anybody using contact lenses. Use ear protectors when utilizing loud power tools. Some tools run at sound levels that damage hearing.

Take care of loose hair and clothes so that it does not get captured in tools; roll your sleeves up and get rid of jewelry. Keep tools out of the reach of kids.

The appropriate respirator or face mask ought to be used when sanding, sawing, or utilizing compounds with harmful fumes. Oily rags are spontaneously flammable, so be careful when you keep and discard them.

Keep blades sharp. A dull blade needs extreme force and can slip which triggers mishaps.

Constantly utilize the appropriate tool for the task. Repair or dispose of tools with fractures in the wood handles or chips in the metal parts.

Do not drill, shape or saw anything that isn't strongly secured. Do not abuse your tools.

Do not work with tools when you are tired. That's when most incidents take place. Do not work with tools when you have actually been utilizing alcohol. Alcohol can warp your judgment. Wait to celebrate after you have actually completed your job! Do not smoke around combustible items like stains and solvents.

Read the owner's handbook for all tools and comprehend their correct use. Disconnect all power tools when changing settings or parts.

Take special care concerning using the table saw fence settings and the tips on how to make cuts utilizing safety guards, push sticks, push blocks, fence straddlers, and feather boards.

The most effective tool in your store is your brain, utilize it. Thinking your cuts and motions through prior to acting can assist in saving both fingers and scrap wood. Take notice of your actions. Looking up to view the store TV or visitor can lead to your hand getting in touch with the blade. Constantly wait up until you have actually finished your cut before you take your eyes off the blade.

Remember that this is simply a pastime and take a break when you feel hurried or annoyed with a project. Mistakes occur when we hurry to finish a task. If your saw is withstanding the cut, stop and see what's wrong. A misaligned rip fence or poorly seated throat plate can often trigger a board to get stuck mid-cut. Pushing the board in these scenarios might induce kickback or contact with the blade. Take a minute to examine the circumstance and identify the issue.

Let the tool stop running. Offering the power tool time to unwind after a cut is an often-overlooked security mistake. Even without power, the spinning blade can still do a great deal of damage.

Accidents are brought on by negligence, taking chances, bad judgment, tiredness, and horseplay. Other causes are poor guidelines (not reading handbooks), missing out on guards, inappropriate clothes, malfunctioning devices, inadequate working area, and bad lighting.

A big step in avoiding an accident is acquainting yourself with any brand-new tool prior to utilizing it, read the handbook, do a dry run with the device unplugged. Just utilize a tool or device for its designated function.

If it is a two-person job, do not attempt to do it alone. Wait up until help is offered.

Keep a tidy store. A jumbled store is a mishap waiting to occur. Keeping your store tidy is going to assist in securing you and your tools from danger. Designate where hand tools are kept, sort nails, screws, and other hardware in containers. Sweep up at the end of the day. Solvent fumes and air-borne dust can present health and explosion dangers. Care ought to be taken to guarantee a supply of fresh air and utilize just explosion-proof vent fans.

Just as there are safety treatments you ought to follow, it assists if you understand the most typical blunders newbies make when starting their wood projects.

Chapter 7: Typical Mistakes

The single most typical mistake in any DIY project is the failure to read and follow the maker's guidelines for any tool or material being utilized. Other typical mistakes consist of taking the safety measures that are set out for a job for granted, and bad project preparation. Here is a list of tips to effectively finish the project properly.

Follow the "Golden Rule" of measuring: "Measure two times, cut once." And offer yourself a lot of time for each step.

Comprehend your strategy. Whether it's a pre-made strategy you bought or downloaded, make certain you understand the actions you need to take to complete the project. Do not be too strict, nevertheless. Be willing to change your strategies if required to complete the piece in such a way that's most convenient for you.

Do not overlook your tools and equipment. Ensure you look after them with cleaning and upkeep regularly. Guarantee that metal surface areas are without rust and blades are kept sharp.

Utilize a sharp pencil or marking knife to make layout marks on your wood. You need to have the ability to see your markings in order to finish the piece properly.

Utilize the identical measuring tape throughout your entire project. Sadly, measuring tapes aren't produced to be accuracy-measuring devices. The hook on the end slides to make up for its own density when shifting between hooking it on the outside of something being measured and pressing it versus the interior of something for an interior measurement. Stay clear of utilizing the hook on the end. Attempt to begin at the one-inch mark, however, keep in mind to deduct that additional inch for the proper measurement.

The second and essential thing is to utilize the identical measuring tape for every single measurement in the project. This is going to counteract the variations between tapes. And if you do utilize the hook, utilize it for ALL the measurements.

Do not cut all the parts out at the same time and anticipate to have an assembling party with the pieces. This is a typical beginner mistake and ought to be stayed away from. Why? The initial reason is that there could be mistakes in the pattern or plan. If you cut out all of the parts initially, and there is more than one mistake, you are going to have a number of good quality pieces of fire wood available for the winter season! It is much better to do things in phases and learn that the plan is filled with errors initially.

The 2nd issue is with wood motion. Modifications in humidity and temperature level can trigger the wood to warp after being cut. This is going to impact all of your joinery. The very best method to combat this is to break the undertaking down into phases.

The next part is going to look at some standard joints to join pieces of wood together.

Chapter 8: Joints

You can have a more finished and professional look to your work by utilizing joints instead of screws and nails. Here are a few of the fundamental joints utilized in woodworking.

Butt Joints

The butt joint is the easiest of the woodworking joints and is really simple for novices to master. The joint includes 2 board ends that are pressed, or butted together and held with nails, screws or glue. Easy wood boxes are typically built with butt joints. While the butt joint provides a fast finish, it does not provide structural strength for the most part. If a butt joint held together with nails is needed to bear much weight, the nails might quickly pull out of the wood. For novices, however, the butt joint provides a simple way to finish a task without costly tools or thorough woodworking understanding.

Dowel Joints

This strategy is perfect for joining 2 flat pieces together to form a bigger flat surface area.

Take 2 pieces of equivalent length wood. Choose now which side is going to be the top and which the bottom for each piece and mark the top side of each so that you do not forget.

Clamp both pieces together, one on top of the other, with the bottoms face to face in the middle. When clamping, guarantee that the two surface areas along which you intend to join these pieces of wood are leveled with one another.

Draw the line down the middle of each surface area to be joined. This need to be precisely the identical on both pieces of wood, otherwise when they are joined there are going to be a step at the join. When this line has actually been drawn, utilize a set square and mark lines throughout the grain of the wood. The intersection of the length and width lines is going to reveal where the dowel holes are going to be drawn.

There is no set guideline for the number of dowels ought to be utilized. Nevertheless, the heavier the weight of whatever is going to be on the surface area, the more dowels ought to be utilized. Usually, one dowel per foot is a great guideline (with a minimum of 2).

As soon as these lines have been drawn, you can then continue to drill the holes at the marked intersections. The drill bit utilized ought to match the size of the dowel being utilized, therefore guaranteeing a tight fit.

When it comes to the dowel itself, you can either make your own little dowels from a longer length, or you can purchase dowel made particularly for this reason. The latter choice is a far superior solution, as the little dowels are beveled at the ends to make it simpler to but them in the holes, and are ribbed to permit the glue to bond more effectively. Each hole ought to be simply over half as deep as the length of the dowel being utilized.

As soon as the holes have actually been drilled, glue one end of each dowel into the holes in the initial piece of wood. Then place glue along the full length of the second piece, making sure that some glue falls into each of the holes.

Unclamp the two pieces and press them together, making sure that the two leading markings are facing up. When done, you ought to clamp securely overnight. Take care when you clamp them to ensure that both pieces stay flat and do not attempt to wrap upwards. To prevent this, it might be essential to clamp the whole piece down to a flat surface area.

Dovetail Joints

The dovetail joint is potentially the very best joint that you can utilize to join 2 pieces of wood together at an appropriate angle. Not just is it a really strong joint, however, it additionally contributes to the appeal of the woodworking project.

The easiest method to produce dovetail joints is to utilize a router and a dovetail template jig. The latter is readily available from any great home enhancement shop and can cost as little as $70. It's well worth the financial investment if you intend to do lots of dovetail joints in the future.

Set up the 3 pieces of the drawer or box and mark the within and beyond each piece. In addition, mark the ends of each piece as it is vital that when cutting the dovetails, the right two ends are cut in one go.

Clamp the front of the drawer and one side into the dovetail device as it follows: the left side of the drawer ought to be clamped under the front clamp (pointing upwards towards the template) with the within the drawer pointing out; the front of the drawer - once again with the interior pointing out - ought to be clamped under the leading clamp so that it butts up against the left drawer.

These 2 pieces ought to be staggered a little, instead of being lined up precisely. The accurate measurement is going to rely on the particular dovetail device that you are utilizing, and this range is going to be provided with its handbook. Nevertheless, it ought to be approximately in the region of 7/16 inch.

When all is firmly clamped in place, utilize the router to cut around the template, following the instructions of the arrows in this diagram.

You can then join the boards together at the joints securing with glue and clamping overnight.

It is well worth experimenting with scrap wood prior to attempting the above procedure on any undertaking as it is going to take a while to get the precise dimensions (like the depth of the router cut) right.

If the joint is too loose, increase the depth of the router cut a little. If the joint is too tight (keep in mind that you still need to squeeze some glue into the joint), slightly reduce the depth of the cut.

Slotted Tenon Joints

Slotted tenon joints are normally utilized as an approach of fixing shelving into a unit's rack walls. Nevertheless, it can additionally be utilized for a variety of other functions.

The concept of a slotted tenon joint is that only one of the two pieces of wood has to be customized in order to achieve a great, tight fit. To do this, one piece has a slot made into it that is the same width as the density of the second piece of wood. This latter piece of wood can then be pressed into the groove, making a strong, right-angled join.

The most reliable method of developing the groove (or slot) is to utilize a router. Although a chisel could be utilized, the quality of the surface is not going to be the same (and it takes far longer to create).

Beware when making the slot to make sure that it is not too large, otherwise, the joint is not going to be tight enough to work. It is far much better to start with too tight of a groove, and after that, expand it.

A router is not constantly the very best tool to utilize, nevertheless. If the groove is to hold a piece of 1/4 inch (or tinier) plywood, you ought to utilize a circular saw rather, altering the depth of cut to as little as 1/4 inch. This tinier cut is perfect when creating the joint for a back panel of a cabinet, like a bedside cabinet.

Now that you have some standard information, let's begin with that initial undertaking!

Chapter 9: Starting With Your Journey

A great location to start is to recognize the sort of wood project you want to try. It could be as basic and helpful as a cutting board with an initial shape, or a birdhouse, or a candle holder for the mantle, or a kid's toy.

You can discover ideas all over for woodworking projects. Maybe you wish to increase the quantity of storage in your home with an easy cabinet. Maybe your kid's toys are simply all over, and you desire a toy box to keep them in. The possibilities are limitless!

Get ideas online. Purchase woodworking publications and check out the projects they have. Get motivated by things you see at craft fairs and flea markets. Attempt to replicate that antique telephone stand you saw. Simply do not attempt to handle anything too complex, or otherwise, you're liable to become annoyed and stop before you even begin.

As a starting woodworker, you ought to select a simple project. Assembling an armoire may not be the very best beginning project. Here are some good plans to get started.

Storage Chest

This chest was created to have a dual function: first of all (and most clearly) as a storage unit, and second of all, as a coffee table in a little living room. The shape is extremely basic, however, it is the most functional for keeping toys and games inside.

In order to enhance the visual appeal of the chest, dovetail joints would be utilized to join the sides. Details of how to develop simple dovetail joints have actually been included in the Joints part. Nevertheless, it is not required to utilize dovetail joints: any kind of jointing, like dowel joints or butt joints, could be utilized.

Construction: The base unit

The sides of the base piece were made out of pine with the front and back being of dimensions 30 x 9 x 3/4 inches and the sides 16 x 9 x 3/4.

Having actually cut these pieces to size, the initial task is to develop the dovetail joints. These are done utilizing a router and a dovetail template (see joints part for more details) with the dovetail showing on the side pieces, not on the front and rear.

As soon as the dovetails have actually been cut, the next task is to develop a way of connecting the base wood into the front and sides. The base was constructed out of a piece of 1/2 inch thick plywood. To connect the base plywood to the sides and front, a slotted tenon joint was cut 1/2 inch from the bottom of the sides, back and front. The size of this slot is 1/2 inch large (the same as the density of the plywood) and 3/8 inch deep.

The size of the base plywood is 29 1/2 inches long by around 16 inches broad. It is necessary that you take your own exact measurement of this piece once you have actually cut the dovetails as the specific dimensions are going to depend upon the depth of the joint. To determine this size, dry-fit the 4 sides together and measure the dimensions of the interior of the box. Then add on a measurement of 3/8 inch at every end for the depth of the slotted tenon joint.

When you have actually cut the base to size, glue the 4 sides and the base together and clamp for numerous hours, making sure that the sides are at 90-degree angles to the front and rear pieces.

The lid

The lid is built in an extremely comparable way. Cut out the front and back to the dimensions 30 x 5 x 3/4 inch, and the sides 16 x 5 x 3/4 inch and path out the dovetails. Take a minute to guarantee that you are cutting the dovetails out of the sides (as you did on the base unit) instead of the front and back.

Unlike the base unit, you do not have to route out a slot for the lid. Rather, the lid is made from pine, of rough dimensions 30 x 16 x 3/4 inches. Once again, take your own measurement by dry fitting the 4 sides. Certainly, to create a piece that is 16 inches broad, you are going to have to join 2 pieces of pine together by doweling them.

Glue the 4 sides together, and after that, glue the top on. There is no requirement for screws or nails. Merely utilize strong wood glue and leave the entire unit clamped overnight.

Completing the task

Sand the whole chest, taking additional care to ensure that all of the corners are nicely rounded off - the last thing you desire are sharp corners that you might bang your leg into - and after that wax it.

Include 2 hinges to the rear of the unit and a clasp to the front. In this project, it is worth purchasing decorative hinges and a clasp as it contributes to the design - concealing the hinges is going to make the chest appear rather dull.

Lastly, include a chain or comparable mechanism to the interior of the chest to stop the lid from swinging open too far, and subsequently harming the hinges.

If you are going to be utilizing this for a toy box, please use non-latching hinges to stay clear of any accidents. They create bounce back hinges that are available at the majority of hardware shops, which are ideal for toy boxes.

A Workbench

This workbench is easy to construct and strong, so it is not going to move around as you work on it. It is additionally little enough to fit in many workshops.

You'll require (Item and Dimensions):

A. Top (198 x 48 x 1800mm)

B. Corner brackets (90 x 35 x 240mm)

C. Side top rails (148 x 48 x 800mm)

D. Front/back top rails (90 x 35 x 1400mm)

E. Coach bolts, nuts and washers (5/16 x 4 1/2 5/16 x 6 ½).

F. Side bottom rails (90 x 35 x 800mm).

G. Legs (98 x 98 x 900mm).

H. Front/back bottom rails (90 x 35 x 1400mm).

I. Shelf (800 x 1470 x 19mm).

J. Bench stop (90 x 35 x 300mm).

Tools

Claw hammer (570g).

Smoothing plane (no. 4).

Marking gauge.

Combination square.

Steel tape (3 meters).

Three beveled-edge firmer chisels (10mm, 18mm, 32mm).

Cross-cut saw (650mm long).

Tenon saw (300mm long).

Nail punch (3mm).

Set of twist drills.

Set of screwdrivers (slotted, pozi, Phillips).

Oil stone.

Sanding cork.

Variable-speed power drill.

Jigsaw

Circular saw.

Here's how:

1. Cut to length the 4 legs (G) and note in housings for leading and bottom rails (D and H). The top housing is 148mm x 48mm deep; the lower one 90mm x 35mm deep. Put your circular saw to the appropriate depth and cut on the waste side of the lines you labeled. Cut a sequence of parallel lines

about 12mm apart between the housing marks and knock out waste. Smooth every housing with a chisel or rasp.

2. Cut to length front and back top and bottom rails (D and H), align them in their housing and pin in place with nails. Drill through both legs and rails and bolt rails to legs. Examine the frame is square by measuring the diagonals.

3. Cut and clamp side rails (C and F) to the front and back frame, then drill and place the longer bolts. Tighten up all nuts firmly and check that the table does not rock.

4. Cut out 4 corner brackets (B) with 45-degree angles. A miter saw is going to be beneficial for this or you can set a circular saw to cut at 45 degrees. Screw brackets in place flush with the top of rails. At this phase, the bench frame ought to be entirely firm.

5. Cut the bottom shelf (I) to fit the dimensions of the bench. Notch out 35mm x 133mm in every corner to clear the legs. The shelf could be screwed in place or left loose.

6. Cut the 5 pieces for the top (A). Move them around to get an excellent fit for the edges and hold them in place with a nail. Screw them to the bench frame with 100mm screws, 2 in every end, sunk somewhat beneath the surface. Utilize a plane to smooth any significant irregularities.

7. Prepare a bench stop (J) as displayed in the detail. Discover the center and measure 60mm and 200mm from one end of a length of 90mm x 35mm pine. Drill an 8mm diameter hole at these points. Draw 2 lines joining the holes and cut along lines with a jigsaw to create a slot. Smooth the cut with a file or sharp chisel. Bevel the end at 45 degrees. Cut bench to a length of 300mm.

8. Find the bench stop where you desire it. Right-handed individuals normally choose the stop at the left-hand end of the bench and left-handed individuals vice-versa. Make certain you stay away

from the braces. Hold the bench stop versus the front rails and mark around it on the underside of the benchtop. Transfer this shape to the top of the bench.

Drill 2 holes in opposite corners and cut out the rectangle-shaped hole. Put in the bench stop and make certain it moves smoothly. Adjust with a file or chisel as required. Hold the bench stop, so it is flush with the benchtop and drill a hole through the front rail at the top of the slot. Place a carriage bolt with a washer and wing nut to enable the bench stop to be raised and dropped easily.

9. Workbenches are generally not finished with paint or a clear finish as it might mark other items which are developed on the bench.

Lastly, let's take a look at a plan for some basic shelving units that could be created quickly!

Chapter 10: What if Something Goes Wrong

Among the initial obstacles a brand-new woodworker needs to get past is the worry of botching a job, and among the very best methods to deal with that apprehension is to merely "think outside the box." The majority of novices choose to begin with something easy (but might not know which projects have easy joinery), and after that, they set out on a hunt for preprinted plans to create such-and-such.

It can end up being aggravating if personal aid is not available. There are a number of methods to cure this, however here is one that has actually worked for numerous folks: forget other people's plans. Design what you require yourself. It isn't as difficult as one may believe, due to the fact that there is constantly some sort of restricting criteria to start with.

A bookshelf should be 10" deep, so the books are going to move into it, and rack spacing is going to match the height of your highest books, plus one inch for finger room. A curio rack is going to be sized by the space available to accommodate it, or by the objects on it. Bed frames ought to fit basic mattress sizes and doors.

The point is, do not hesitate to start these projects by yourself. There is a huge knowledge base of woodworking insight available in print and online. If the undertaking does not end up as you'd intended, you can always start over, and you are going to have learned a lot along the way. We frequently discover more from our mistakes in working wood than from easy successes.

Why not attempt to develop your own piece? Drawing ideas out freehand on paper is useful. What if it were in this manner, or in that manner? Hand sketches are going to reveal to you how ideas can come together, or clash with one another. Then, if you understand that the shelf needs to fit an area 5 feet high in general, the variety of shelves to include are going to be determined by the height of the items to be put there. Heavy or bigger items (or spaces) normally go near the bottom of a unit, to anchor it physically in addition to the eye when seen from the end of a room. Spaces can additionally be separated.

Designs can additionally be planned based upon what wood a woodworker might have available. If you have a number of 2x4s sitting around, an Early American or pinewood appearance might be required. Be sure to thoroughly square up any stock. Construction castoffs are quickly ripped to functional dimensions on a table saw, however, learn the safety procedures for your device prior to attempting to rip longboards.

Creating your own project can additionally imply adapting somebody else's plan to your own usage. It's rather typical for a woodworker to see the perfect blanket chest, couch table or display case, and after that, think "But I want mine to be ..." and revamp the whole structure. Do not hesitate to trust your impulses and be creative when making a piece. Educate yourself; ask questions on online woodworking forums or at clubs and guilds. You'll quickly amaze yourself with just how much you can do.

CONCLUSION

There are numerous, numerous locations where you can locate patterns for your own woodworking undertakings. There are lots of locations online. Do not forget your local library, along with home enhancement shops like Lowe's and Home Depot. These locations hold a substantial line of house woodworking plans for you to finish and wow your friends and family.

Keep in mind the safety procedures laid out in this book. You can not be too cautious when it concerns keeping yourself safe in your workroom. When you deal with power tools and even hand tools, mishaps can occur that can impact you in dreadful ways. This book is filled with instructions and recommendations; the rest is up to you!

The fulfillment you can discover when you take up woodworking as a pastime can be fantastic. You are not going to believe the pride you feel as you explain to visitors to your house that you created a furniture piece yourself.

Simply keep in mind to take your time, be safe, and take pride in your work! After all, it was created by you with the two hands you were provided. What could be more gratifying than that?

I hope that you enjoyed reading through this book and that you have found it useful. If you want to share your thoughts on this book, you can do so by leaving a review on the Amazon page. Have a great rest of the day.

Printed in Great Britain
by Amazon

43261595R00047